Bible Lessons with Babies

Emily Hoffhines

Bible Lessons with Babies
ISBN 978-0-6151-7178-4

Copyright © 2007 by Emily Hoffhines
All rights reserved

Scripture quotations taken from
the New American Standard Bible®,
Copyright © 1960, 1962, 1963, 1968, 1971, 1972, 1973,
1975, 1977, 1995 by The Lockman Foundation
Used by permission. (www.Lockman.org)

cover photo by Miles Hoffhines

Hear, O Israel! The LORD is our God, the LORD is one! You shall love the LORD your God with all your heart and with all your soul and with all your might. These words, which I am commanding you today, shall be on your heart. You shall teach them diligently to your sons and shall talk of them when you sit in your house and when you walk by the way and when you lie down and when you rise up.
Deuteronomy 6:4-7

The purpose, the plan, and the procedure for the essentials of parenting are all laid out in these few verses. The purpose is to love, the plan is to teach, and the procedure is to live. Living is daily. It is happening in the present. It is happening all around us. It is in our sitting, our walking, our lying down, and our rising up.

In *Bible Lessons with Babies*, small milestones that are passed in everyday life become object lessons which show us the extraordinary nature of God infused into ordinary everyday living. While Baby discovers the physical world around him, parents rediscover how spiritual reality is integrated into daily life.

Babies are designed by their Creator to receive their most powerful training through everyday living. *Bible Lessons with Babies* helps put a context of purpose into their achievements. Routine opportunities to recognize God in life's simple things are often missed because they *are* routine. The game-like qualities of these exercises build times of shared affection. Deep relationships built on the common places of our lives have the greatest influence. God's deepest truths are established in the language of life.

Table of Contents

Early Babyhood 9
A New Life, A New Love...11
Sweet Sleep 12
Perfect Praise I 13
Cuddles According to Solomon..14
Dancing For Joy...15
Jesus Is the Light 16
Marching 17
Linking Sight and Sound I 18
Happy Talk 19
Reach Out 20
Hokey, But Not Pokey 21
Mirror Images 22
Light...23
Perfect Praise II..24
Bubbles 25
Linking Sight and Sound II 26

Middle Babyhood 27
Faces 29
Shake, Rattle, and Rejoice 30
Push Ups 31
Just for Kicks 32
Something to Sink My Teeth Into 33
Peek-A-Who 34
Make A Joyful Noise 35
Roll Away 36
Horsey Ride 37
Nonsense! 38
The Great Escape...39
Taking a Turn 40
What A Bang! 41
See Hunt...42
In A Pinch 43
Imitation...44
Pull-ups 45
Shining Faces...46
Water Baby 47

 Late Babyhood 49
Bookworm 51
Stringing Along 52
Shape and Form 53
Echo 54
Accuracy 55
Where Is It? 56
It's A Ball 57
Good Measure 58
The Shell Game 59
No Other Name 60
Expectation 61
Taking a stand 62
Bye-bye 63

 Appendix 65

How to use this Book

Each lesson contains three elements; an exercise or activity for Baby, a corresponding principle or precept from the Holy Bible, and a verse of scripture. The purpose of combining these elements is not to teach Baby new skills or to reveal new and deeper insight, although that may happen incidentally. The chief purpose is to practice a God-awareness in common everyday activity.

For ease of use, Baby's exercises are separated in to early, middle and late periods of Baby's first year. Since all babies develop at their own individual mental and physical rates, the suggested age is merely a general guide. The lessons do not have to be done in order.

Many of the precepts covered in the object lessons are things students of the Bible will be aware of already; but what is new is the perspective of how God's word crops up in and is infused into the little events of life.

A related verse of scripture ends every lesson. Reflecting or meditating on this will lead to new perspectives on familiar principles.

Perhaps the most important benefit is that Baby will gain experience interacting with an adult who is consciously bringing the Spirit of Christ into their life's activities day after day. This is building a foundation that will last a lifetime.

Early Babyhood

A New Life, A New Love

Newborn

No equipment

Welcoming a new baby into our family, our home, and our hearts once again sets in motion the Lord's great commission: making disciples of all men. (Matthew 28:19) Here is a new soul to teach.

New parents expect a baby to transform their schedules, their financial decisions, their image and dreams. A baby also alters the nature of our approach to the commission of making new disciples because the task becomes incredibly and indelibly personal. Birth made it unmistakably evident that Baby has a body; and with it came the awesome realization that Baby is a spiritual being who has a soul. For a season, he is ours to protect and to train; and conceivably to love for eternity.

Every noble enterprise ought to begin by connecting with the Creator. Bringing up children in the power, instruction, and love of the Lord is one of the noblest passages of life. It is fitting then, that we begin by prayer.

We pray:
> Watch over your heart with all diligence
> For from it flow the springs of life. Proverbs 4:23

Sweet Sleep

Newborn

Equipment: crib, rocking chair

Sleep comes so naturally to newborns; they don't have to be taught how to do it. Nothing is quite so sweet as rocking a baby to sleep. A loving atmosphere helps a child grow well, but a peaceful atmosphere helps a child relax.

All children, and particularly newborns, take their cues from their parents. When the parent is stressed out, the baby is more likely to fuss. When the parent is unruffled, the child feels more secure. The same principle pertains to our spiritual lives. When we recognize God as the One who controls the universe, when we worship Him as our shield and defender, when we praise Him as our shelter and citadel; then our own lives become less frantic and more restful. The tranquility of a sleeping child exemplifies the contentment to be found in the serenity of God.

In peace will I both lie down and sleep,
For thou alone, O Lord, dost make me to dwell in safety. Psalm 4:8

Perfect Praise I

Newborn and up

No equipment

    Praise is both an action and attitude of the heart. Even the youngest child will respond to praise. Let the room be filled with an atmosphere of praise toward Jesus by lifting up your voice in song or by playing melodic hymns of praise. A small baby has many physical limitations, but his spirit is receptive to praise.

    Often we think of praise as an excited expression of our delight, but there also exists a quieter form of praise that bears the joys of contentment. It is this softer form of praise that can quiet a fussy baby or calm a tired cry.

    Quiet praise will calm and refresh our spirits and position us to better hear the small nuances and subtle distinctions the Lord wants to show us. Quiet praise helps shut out the cares of the world.

Great is the Lord, and highly to be praised,
And His greatness is unsearchable.
One generation shall praise Your works to another,
And shall declare Your mighty acts.
        Psalm 145:3,4

Cuddles According to Solomon

Newborn

No equipment

> Song of Solomon 2:4b, 6
>> His banner over me is love
>> Let his left hand be under my head
>> And his right hand embrace me.

This scripture draws a perfect picture of holding a baby. One hand is supporting the newborn's head. The other is giving a secure and gentle hug. Babies need lots of cuddling; at this age it's nearly impossible to give them too much. Jesus himself held children in his arms. As you are cuddling, speak words of blessing and love over Baby.

The scripture is also a perfect illustration of how God holds the human soul, and in turn, of how we ought to handle the souls of others: with supportive sustaining love. The left hand of justice is supportive, while the right hand of honor is sustaining. The two hands work together in a balanced love that upholds integrity and embraces appreciation.

And He took them in his arms and began blessing them and laying his hands on them. Mark 10:16

Dancing For Joy

Newborn and up

Equipment: music player or you voice

In the dance, thankfulness, praise, and tributes are joyfully expressed as a harmonization of the senses: sight, sound, touch, and even scent. Miriam led the women in a dance to praise God after the triumph of the Red Sea crossing. (Exodus 15:20, 21) David danced when the Ark of the Lord was brought into Jerusalem. (II Samuel 6:14, 15) Jephthah's daughter danced as he returned from the battle in victory. (Judges 11:34)

Dancing initiates Baby into the joys of praise. Hold him closely, supporting his head securely as it rests on your shoulder. Add sweet music and gentle swaying movements. If you use recorded music, sing or hum along with the song; the baby will feel the vibrations of your singing and it will increase his sense of well-being.

The dancing in the Bible has almost nothing to do with any modern concept of date-night fun. Most often, the dance was an expression of gratitude for a triumph in battle or a safe return of a warrior. The joy of the dance had its roots in gratefulness.

Let them praise his name with dancing. Psalm 149:3

Jesus Is the Light

2 months old and up

Equipment: penlight or small flashlight (not a laser pointer)

The first words God spoke during the Genesis creation were to declare, "Let there be light!" It is fitting then, that one of the first things to attract Baby's attention is lights. Move the penlight in slow easy patterns. Watch as Baby's eyes follow it. Very young babies will focus best at a distance of 8-10". As the eye muscles develop, move back to 12-14". Moving the light from side to side is easiest for the baby to follow; up and down is a little harder, and around in circles is harder still. Practice both clock- and counterclockwise circles. Then try figure eights.

As adults, the Lord does not always lead us in a straight line either. We are constantly challenged to keep our eyes on Him to see where his next move will be. As you help Baby to develop his own eye muscle coordination, let your heart be renewed to the importance of keeping you focus on Jesus.

I am the light of the world. John 8:12

Marching

2 months old and up

No equipment, music optional

The Old Testament is full of accounts of conquests of the armies of Israel whenever they were directed by God; and of defeats when they refused to listen to him.

For this exercise have Baby lie on his back. Take one of his feet in each of your hands, pushing one hand up gently so Baby's knees bends up towards his chest; then bring his leg back down to starting position. Alternate sides so you are moving his legs as if he were "marching." This will not only improve flexibility, but the repetitive alternating motion also stimulates brain activity.

Similarly, we need both flexibility and an alert mind in order to walk in the ways of the Lord. Consider your goals for Baby and for yourself. Marching toward a victory, unlike aimless wandering or a casual stroll, has both direction and purpose.

They run like mighty men, they climb the wall like soldiers and they each march in line, nor do they deviate from their paths. Joel 2:7

Linking Sight and Sound I

As early as 2 months; peak interest around four months

Equipment: rattle or squeaky toy

    Babies begin exploring right from birth. Early visual training exercises will help babies become good observers as they explore God's earth.

    Begin by holding a rattle about 10 inches in front of Baby's eyes and shake it very gently. Once Baby has focused on it, begin moving the rattle to the side of his field of vision. Watch to see how his eyes follow it. Very young babies will move their eyes in jerky movements as they try to track a moving object. Their ability to follow motion will become smoother as Baby grows.

    Place the rattle in Baby's hand. Young babies may not be able to hold it for very long but he will experience what it feels like to grasp an object and eventually he'll figure out that he is causing the rattling sound by moving. Alternate hands to give Baby practice on both sides.

    Our ability to keep our eyes on God and to see where He is moving also takes some practice, yet it is important to develop this skill so that we can handle the things God gives us without dropping them.

The hearing ear and the seeing eye,
    The Lord has made both of them. Proverbs 20:12

Happy Talk

As early as 2½ months, better results at 4-5 months

No equipment

    We know that laughter is a good thing. Proverbs 17:22 tells us that a cheerful heart is like good medicine; and studies have shown a correlation between happiness and good mental health. Merriment and rejoicing should be an integral part of our daily lives. Encourage Baby to smile by smiling at him. Talk to him in a pleasant tone. Create an atmosphere of joy around you by rejoicing.

    Find an encouraging Bible verse and say it to Baby. Repeat it again and again. It does not matter if he doesn't understand it as long as you do. The spoken Word will produce joy; when you have such joy overflowing from your own heart, your baby will pick up on it. Like a cheerleader at a sporting event, you build an atmosphere of confidence around Baby and strengthen yourself at the same time.

Then our mouth was filled with laughter And our tongue with joyful shouting... The LORD has done great things for us; We are glad.
    Psalm 126:2a, 3

Reach Out

3 months

Equipment: plastic Slinky® or dangling toy

    Prop Baby up in a reclining seat or lay him on his back in a protected area. Dangle the toy at a distance where Baby must swipe his hand, bat his arm, or kick his legs to reach it. Start by suspending the Slinky above the center of Baby's body. As his coordination improves, move the toy around to a variety of angles and distances. Talk to Baby during this activity to encourage him to reach for the toy. Allow him to catch it often enough to keep interest in the game.

    The simple act of reaching out incorporates several areas which have counterparts in ministry: there is an effort put forth, a contact made, and a goal attained. Notice that the act of reaching out is a response to having first seen a desirable object. If we see God and his kingdom as desirable, then we ought to be making a vigorous effort to reach him.

Brethren, I do not regard myself as having laid hold of it yet; but one thing I do: forgetting what lies behind and reaching forward to what lies ahead, I press on toward the goal for the prize of the upward call of God in Christ Jesus. Philippians 3:13, 14

Hokey, But Not Pokey

3 months through walking

Equipment: blanket, clean rug, or floor pad

Here is an action song you can sing and play with Baby.
Sing to the tune of *Hokey-Pokey*

You lift your left arm up	*lift baby's left arm*
You put your left arm down	*bring baby's arm back down*
You lift your left arm up	*lift baby's left arm again*
Then we shake it all around	*shake arm gently*
And rub your little tummy	*rub baby's tummy*
'Cause Jesus is sweet as honey	*rub reverse direction*
Ears and cheeks and nose	*touch ears, cheeks, and nose*

Other verses: right arm, left leg, right leg, elbow, knee, etc.

  This is an enjoyable way to remind ourselves that the Lord's plan for His church is to have all its 'body parts' working together in harmony.

For even as the body is one and yet has many members, and all the members of the body, though they are many, are one body, so also is Christ. I Corinthians 12:12

Mirror Images

As early as 3 months, peak interest around 7-9 months

Equipment: non-breakable metal mirror

Genesis 1:26 tells us that God made man in his image and likeness. That is a wonderful thought for meditation. Babies often show a keen interest in examining their own images in a mirror. Hold or position a non-breakable mirror where baby can see himself. Older babies may want to hold the mirror themselves. Speak distinctly and point out the different parts of the face: nose, cheek, mouth, etc.

Man was created in the image of God. After the fall of Adam, we all became candidates for some radical plastic surgery of the heart. Jesus is our promise and our means of return to the image we were meant for. Our salvation by faith is instantaneous, yet the restoration of the image of God in us is gradual and progressive.

Baby's image will change as he grows. Our image should also be growing as we conform our own spirit to the image of Christ.

But we all, with unveiled face, beholding as in a mirror the glory of the Lord, are being transformed into the same image from glory to glory, just as from the Lord, the Spirit. II Corinthians 3:18

Light

3 months and up

Equipment: a penlight

In *Jesus Is the Light* (2 months), Baby was following the light's movement up and down and from side to side. Now that baby is more developed, it is time to try a new dimension—depth.

See if baby can track the light all the way across the room. Stand or sit a few feet away from Baby and move the light in patterns of wide circles and figure 8's. You may want to try a quick "dive" towards Baby's nose, but please don't try to make him look cross-eyed for any length of time.

Light is energy. God's first words quite literally energized His creation, and they can energize our mind and spark understanding as well. Proper lighting of an object improves our depth perception. For us to be able to perceive the deeper things of God, we need the light of His revelation.

You will have the Lord for an everlasting light, And your God for your glory. Isaiah 60:19

Perfect Praise II

4 months and up

No equipment

One of the most important things you can ever do is to make God known to the children. A simple and effective way to make God known is to call Baby's attention to Him as part of your lifestyle. In the early morning, tell Baby that God makes the day. At breakfast, thank Him for his provision. You will find many opportunities throughout the day to point out God's creative character.

Scripture is full of similes, metaphors and analogies to describe God. Use the objects your baby sees, touches, and hears to boost both his language development and his emerging knowledge of God.

Here are a few to get you started: God created plants, animals, and of course, dirt. God shines like the sun, refreshes like the rain, and is a shelter in a storm. He's solid like a rock, delightful like a fountain.

They shall speak of the glory of Your kingdom
And talk of Your power;
To make known to the sons of men Your mighty acts
And the glory of the majesty of Your kingdom.
    Psalm 145: 11, 12

Bubbles

4 months and up

Equipment: bubble solution, bubble wand

Blowing bubbles with Baby can be delightfully refreshing and tension-relieving. If another child wants to join in, the fun of bubble blowing can become a social opportunity as well. Make a sport of it either outdoors or at bath time. If you have a leak-proof cap on your bottle this activity is also wonderfully portable so you can pack the supplies and make bubbles on a walk through the park.

When you see Baby enjoying the bubbles, remember how such a few drops of soap film blew out to encompass a large volume of air. We should hope to live like this; where our few words can produce a great delight.

The words of a man's mouth are deep waters;
The fountain of wisdom is a bubbling brook. Proverbs 18:4

Linking Sight and Sound II

4 - 5 months

Equipment: rattle or squeaky toy

This activity is similar to *Linking Sight and Sound I*. This time, hold the toy off to the side just out of his field of vision. Shake the rattle gently so Baby will have to turn his head to find what is making the sound. Repeat on both sides.

God's voice can also come from different directions. It may come from dreams, prophets, visions, thunder, preachers, scripture, or even a burning bush. Hearing God through such external sources doesn't require much from us beyond good judgment to know we are not being deceived. But hearing Him speak to our heart often takes training and practice. This inward witness will bypass all our senses. When God's spirit bears witness with our spirit, there is usually no feeling of emotion, it is usually quiet and without fanfare; it is something we just know. When God lives in us, His voice inside us has the unvoiced sound of a godly intuition.

Your ears will hear a word behind you, "This is the way, walk in it," whenever you turn to the right or to the left. Isaiah 30:21

Middle Babyhood

Faces

5 months

Equipment: Pictures of family members, friends, portraits of Jesus

Babies show a great deal of interest in looking at faces. As they explore the relationship between different facial features; they develop the concept of what a face is. By five months, the nerves and muscles in the eyes can find shape and motion. Now the brain begins processing the more difficult task of trying to identify what it is we are looking at.

Look at pictures of faces with Baby, pointing out and naming their identities and features (lips, eyebrows, chin, etc.) It is our face which makes us recognizable as an individual.

The Bible is full of stories about people who did or did not recognize each other. Isaac mistook Jacob for Esau. Judah failed to recognize Tamar. Joseph recognized his brothers, but they did not recognize him. Saul recognized David; Obadiah recognized Elijah; and the list goes on. It important to know others; it is also important to be known by them. It is comforting to know we are known by God.

Then their offspring will be known among the nations, And their descendants in the midst of the peoples. All who see them will recognize them Because they are the offspring whom the LORD has blessed. Isaiah 61:9

Shake, Rattle, and Rejoice

4-6 months

Equipment: rattle

Deuteronomy 12:7 instructs us to rejoice in all that we put our hand to. We can cheerfully enjoy what our hands produce. In Baby's case this will be a cheery sound. With younger babies, place the rattle in the palm of their hand; or simply offer it to an older baby.

As adults, we should always be looking for the simple joys of life and be aware of ways to demonstrate our thanks. Our moments of rejoicing do not have to wait for a special place and time but we can create them now in the elements of the life that surrounds us.

Rejoicing is a state of the heart, not an emotion of the senses. Life often hands us unpleasant, even wicked things which are not as uncomplicated as a toy rattle. The New Testament gives examples of being able to rejoice in times of famine, Luke 6:23; during times of persecution, Acts 5:41; in imprisonment, Acts 16:25; in the loss of property, Hebrews 10:34; and in fiery trials, 1 Peter 4:12, 13

Rejoice in the Lord always; again I will say, rejoice!   Philippians 4:4

Push Ups

4 – 5 months

Equipment: blanket, clean rug, or a play pad

By now, Baby is staying awake for longer periods of time and taking more interest in his surroundings. Throw a baby blanket down in a spot out of harm's way where Baby can feel a part of what is going on around him and place Baby on his tummy. He will probably try to lift his head up from the blanket in a push-up fashion. Babies who are used to spending a lot of time in child seats and sleeping on their backs may fuss at being put on their tummy, but it is important to strengthen their neck and back muscles and to develop motor-skill control. Placing him in a safe spot where he can observe plenty of action around him will divert his attention from being face down. If baby is struggling, you can place a rolled towel under his chest and armpits for extra support.

The common push-up is a repetition and resistance exercise that builds our strength when our face is down. In the spiritual application, the more we resist sin and iniquity, the more our strength increases.

But You, O LORD, are a shield about me, My glory, and the One who lifts my head. Psalm 3:3

Just for Kicks

4 – 6 months

Equipment: plastic Slinky® or jingle bells

Kicking comes naturally to babies. In this exercise you can encourage Baby to use his legs and feet by dangling a Slinky where he can kick it. Another form of this game is to sew bells on to a pair of booties, but they must be securely attached so that they do not become a choking hazard.

Kicking exercises can also be done at bath time in three or four inches of water. For safety's sake, do the kicking before using soap; both to keep soap from accidentally splashing in Baby's eyes and also to reduce slippery conditions when you are supporting baby.

A kick is a sudden thrust. The common phrase "kick the habit" speaks of booting out undesirable things. When objectionable things try to enter our lives spiritually, we ought to use a sudden thrust to get rid of them, kick them out, and not allow the sin to linger.

Watch the path of your feet, And all your ways will be established. Proverbs 4:26

Something to Sink My Teeth Into

about 5 months plus

Equipment: hard rubber or gel filled teething toy

By five months, some babies will have cut their first tooth and many others will be trying to. Most babies have a God-designed urge to bite or chew when they are teething. This is a good thing because the added pressure helps break down tissue and allows the teeth to come through the gum. One of the best things you can do is to give Baby something safe to chew on. When babies begin exploring objects by putting them in their mouths, it becomes especially important to keep all toys as clean as possible.

Teething is a time of preparation for eating solid food. You will notice that Baby cuts his teeth in order from front to back and balanced symmetrically. As we grow into the solid fare of a Christian life, it too must be done in balance and in order.

Your teeth are like a flock of ewes Which have come up from their washing, All of which bear twins… Song of Solomon 6:6

Peek-A-Who

6 months

Equipment: cheesecloth or tulle, scarf or receiving blanket

God is present, even when we cannot see him. These variations on the game of peek-a-boo help Baby discover that things exist even when they cannot be seen.

In the simplest form of this exercise, play peek-a-boo by cupping your hands over your face. Baby may not see your eyes, but he still sees you. The next stage of this game uses a square of cheesecloth or sheer fabric to hide your face. Baby can partially see you through the cloth, but your face will look different from the face he is used to. Vary the position of your peeking; sometimes over the top, sometimes under the bottom, and sometimes around the side. Finally, use the solid cloth so your face is completely hidden.

Sometimes there are objects in our lives that block our clear view of God. We must learn to trust that he is still there. We will see Him again.

…Nor has He hidden His face from him; But when he cried to Him for help, He heard. Psalm 22:24

Make A Joyful Noise

6 months

Equipment: rattles, chime balls, thick dowel stick, etc. Old coffee cans, margarine bowls, or plastic storage containers with lids make good drums.

Babies choose to make noise! They deliberately make sounds with their toys. In addition to making noise by shaking rattles, try to offer some items that make sounds by pushing rolling or banging. And don't neglect the double-fisted joy; if Baby has one object he will bang it on the table or floor, but with two objects he can bang them together. This all trains his coordination and motor control.

In this verse, people were celebrating the coronation of King Solomon. The exuberance was so great that the earth shook; it was the result of free choice. When Jesus is crowned King of Kings, there will be noisy jubilation. Everyone will be there by choice. From the viewpoint of the King, there is great satisfaction in knowing that his people are devoted to him.

…and the people were rejoicing with great joy, so that the earth shook at their noise. I Kings 1:40

Roll Away

5 - 7 months

Equipment: bath towel

Most babies roll from their tummy onto their back first because it takes more strength to flip from the back over onto their tummy. The ages suggested for this activity differ considerably. Baby's personality and size have as much to do with his skill development as his age does.

Rolling over will happen naturally when Baby's control and strength develop enough for him to able to push up from his shoulders. Place Baby on a clean bath towel. Using both hands, lift one edge a few inches to give Baby a boost sensation of beginning to roll. Some babies have personalities that love this and you can make a game of gently rolling him from side to side on the towel. Other babies find rolling to be a strange sensation and you will need to practice small lifts several times to overcome his wariness.

Serving the Lord sometimes requires the vital skill of being able to turn over and see things from a different position. Blessings become apparent when we shift to God's perspective.

So I will turn toward you and make you fruitful and multiply you, and I will confirm My covenant with you. Leviticus 26:9

Horsey Ride

After Baby can sit

Equipment: sturdy chair for adult

This is a simple activity which almost every child loves. Sit on a chair; have Baby sit on your knees facing you. You may need to hold the hands or forearms of younger babies while older ones will be able to hold onto your thumbs for balance. Bounce him on your knees to give him a horsey ride. Saying a rhyme will match the rhythm of the gait (sense of touch) to the rhythm of the verse (sense of sound.)

> *Clippity cloppity, clippity clop,*
> *God's love will never stop.*
> *Trippity trottity, trippity trot,*
> *Jesus loves you quite a lot.*

Horses are mentioned frequently in the Bible, most often in connection with warfare where soldiers were trained as horsemen. Scripture repeatedly reminds us that we must trust in God, not in horses, for victory on the battlefields of life.

See Psalms 20:7; 33:17; 147:10,11; and Proverbs 21:31

And I saw heaven opened, and behold, a white horse, and He who sat on it is called Faithful and True, and in righteousness He judges and wages war. Revelation 19:11

Nonsense!

6 months and up

No equipment

As a newborn, almost all sounds Baby made were sounds of discomfort— hunger, loneliness, etc. Within a couple months, coos and gurgles became more expressive signals of contentment and may even have been punctuated with squeals of delight. Early babbling sounds are the same, no matter what language the baby is used to hearing. Sometime around seven months, give or take a few weeks, a baby's babbling begins to imitate the tones and patterns of his mother tongue. This is a critical time in language development when babbling is good practice for distinct speech and should be encouraged.

Start imitating a sound Baby already makes naturally. Try to get a "dialogue" going where you and baby take turns speaking gibberish and nonsense sounds. This milestone is called reciprocal babbling. It shows that he has learned to respond to you by using his voice. It usually works best if Baby is facing you and can see your face, mouth, and lips as you talk to him. Compare Baby's effort with your own response to God's voice.

From the mouth of infants and nursing babes You have established strength. Psalm 8:2

The Great Escape

6 months and up

Equipment: short length of colorful wide ribbon or floaty scarf

Psalm 91 talks about the security we can have in the Lord and about our escape from the evil one. The Lord has promised to deliver us from pestilence, terror, and traps that the devil tries to place in our path. In this easy activity, baby learns to escape from a colorful ribbon or scarf. Simply wrap a scarf or wide ribbon <u>loosely</u> once or twice around Baby's arm or foot. Make a game of it as you tug gently on the ribbon and baby tries to break free. Always let him win.

Babies can be easily ensnared by a few inches of fabric. As we mature, we find other forms of traps that bind our soul as well as body. Some snares are of our own making such as worldliness, selfishness, or unbelief. But others, as in this game, come from outside sources. God has given his word that He will answer our call for help and rescue us.

Our soul has escaped as a bird out of the snare of the trapper; The snare is broken and we have escaped. Psalm 124:7

Taking a Turn

7 months

Equipment: an object that attracts Baby's attention

By now, Baby is ready to strengthen and develop muscles that will help him turn his own body. Put Baby on his stomach and attract his attention by holding an item in front of him but just beyond his reach. As soon as he spots it, move it off to his side. Try to encourage Baby to pivot on his stomach in order to keep the item in view. Practice turning both clockwise and counterclockwise turns. Let him reach the toy before he become too frustrated.

Life is filled with good things to turn towards and bad things to turn from. As you play with Baby, pray for him that he will turn to Jesus as he grows and matures. Then do a quick check of your own life. What things get your attention? Are they important things you should turn toward? Are they trivial or injurious things you should turn from?

Turn to Me and be saved, all the ends of the earth; For I am God, and there is no other. Isaiah 45:22

What A Bang!

8 months +

Equipment: cymbals, pot lids, etc. and an unsharpened pencil or wooden spoon to use as your conductor's baton

In earlier activities such as *Shake Rattle and Roll*, and *Make a Joyful Noise*, the emphasis was on producing a sound, any sound, by shaking a rattle, rolling a chime ball, or beating a drum. This is a noisy lesson also, but now the challenge is to have Baby start and stop the banging as he gives a "command performance."

Baby is advancing in an emerging awareness of cause and effect; he knows banging his cymbals will make a sound. Now you can begin working on teaching him to clang the cymbals only on command when you point at him with a stick or baton. This marks a significant move ahead in his development, so you will want to try this when he is alert and being not fussy about other things.

Christians need to be able to listen and act at God's command. Both timing and obedience are important. If we make noise when we ought to be resting, we destroy much of our testimony. If we rest when we ought to be speaking up, we fail to have a testimony.

Praise Him with loud cymbals; Praise Him with resounding cymbals.
Psalm 150:5

See Hunt

8 months

Equipment: small plaything, scarf, plastic bowls, paper

Christians believe in many things they cannot see; angels, heaven, God himself. This activity helps Baby recognize that things do exist even when he cannot see them. Let Baby sit facing you. Take a small object that attracts Baby's interest and try to get him to reach for it. Just before Baby can grab it, toss a square of cloth over it. Does Baby still attempt to get the toy? Or is he now interested in the cloth? Try encouraging him to look for the toy under the scarf. If he readily looks for the toy, try some other types of covers. Baby is on his way to understanding that things exist even when he cannot see them.

Even so, it is easier once they are revealed. The Lord has given his promise that right and wrong, truth and error, even though we may not see them now, will someday be revealed.

"Therefore do not fear them, for there is nothing concealed that will not be revealed, or hidden that will not be known. Matthew 10:26

In A Pinch

9 months

Equipment: bite size cereal rings or bits

"Examine everything carefully; hold fast to that which is good;" declares I Thessalonians 5:21. When Baby did the *Hold Fast* exercise a few months ago, he was still grasping objects with his whole hand, almost as if he were wearing a mitten. By now he will have refined the movement in his fingers and thumb to where he can begin picking up objects by pinching them. Baby's snack time can be a practice session for developing his fine motor skills when you give him small cereal bits or banana slices to feed himself.

When Baby picks up and eats his cereal rings, they strengthen his body. Remember that as you hold fast to the truth of the gospel, to the vigor of grace, and to your love for the body of Christ, you will also be strengthened.

...hold fast what you have, so that no one will take your crown. Revelation 3:11

Imitation

By 9 months

No equipment

Babies learn by imitating what they observe. And it is one of the most practical forms of learning because Baby's entire self is involved. You can easily turn baby's natural inclination to imitate into a game. Here are some ideas to get you started:
- Clap your hands
- Shake your head
- Make "O" lips
- Blink your eyes
- Wiggle your nose
- Wave your hand

Similarly, a practical, straightforward method for developing our own understanding of the nature of God comes by imitation of His kindness, His Forgiveness, and His love.

Therefore be imitators of God, as beloved children. Ephesians 5:1

Pull-ups

About 9 months

No equipment

 This exercise can help strengthen Baby's muscles, but it also demonstrates an important biblical model: That we ought to help pull others up from the devil's snare, and that doing so will help them grow stronger.

 Have Baby lie on his back. If the surface is hard, you may want to add a pillow under his head. Face him and have him grasp your thumbs while you support his wrists with your fingers. Slowly pull Baby up to a sitting position, repeat several times, and speak words of encouragement as you do.

 At this stage, babies are too weak to pull themselves straight up; they have to rely on our help to raise them up from being flat on their back. Many times we have to rely on God or the people He sends to help us move upwards. We have to acknowledge our weaknesses and trust in the strength of the Lord.

You will pull me out of the net which they have secretly laid for me, For You are my strength. Into Your hand I commit my spirit.
 Psalm 31:4

Shining Faces

9 months

Equipment: non-breakable mirror

In *Mirror Images* (3 months), you encouraged Baby to look at himself in a mirror and were reminded that God created man in His image. By now, Baby is ready for a few variations of this simple task. Hold the mirror in front of Baby. Does he smile when he sees himself now? Or does he stare with intense interest? Take the mirror away; what is Baby's reaction? Now position the mirror so that he can see both your face and his own at the same time. Does he watch you or look at himself? See if you can start a mimicking game. Blink your eyes, will Baby blink his? Purse your lips; will Baby purse his? Smile; will Baby smile back?

Envision yourself in your child's place and think about how you respond when the Lord looks in on you. Do you see Him? Or do you continue to focus on yourself? When the Lord smiles on you, do you smile back?

Make Your face to shine upon Your servant... Psalm 31:16

Water Baby

9 months and up

Equipment: a mismatched sock *(a thick cotton sock will make the best washcloth)* and a permanent marker; or use a purchased bath puppet

You can make a bath time puppet from an old sock— two dots for eyes drawn with a permanent marker makes a satisfactory puppet, or you could embroider as fancy a face as you wish. Have fun with Baby as you make the puppet chomp or nibble the soap and then either attack or kiss, (depending upon the puppet's personality,) those dirty feet and hands.

The Bible has much to say about cleanliness and much of the Levitical law deals with public health and personal hygiene issues. Cleanness may relate to attitudes and motives behind human behavior. In still another usage, it applies to the human condition: mankind's fall and the need to be cleansed from sin. The New Testament teaches that the blood of Jesus His Son cleanses us from all sin.

One of the most beautiful expressions of cleanliness is found in David's prayer of Psalm 51. This cleanness is a new creation which comes only from the power of God.

Create in me a clean heart, O God, And renew a steadfast spirit within me. Psalm 51:10

Late Babyhood

Bookworm

10 months

Equipment: board and cloth books

By ten months old, the average baby has developed enough coordination between his eyes, his intellect, and his hands that he can begin to enjoy books. If he has not been introduced to them already, now is a great time to start. Use sturdy books so that Baby can turn the pages himself. Don't be upset if he is more interested in turning the pages than in looking at the pictures at first. Once that Baby becomes familiar with how pages turn, he'll settle down and begin looking at the pictures. Young babies will likely show a more active response to your pointing to and naming the pictured object than they will to reading the story or text. But do both. Reading the simple stories will give Baby a feel for the flow of language even if he does not fully understand what is being read.

From before the time of Abraham, the written word has been important in recording the deeds, the ways, and the will of God. We should approach the Holy Bible with the anticipation of an explorer. Each new discovery lets our heart cry, "Eureka!"

"Behold, I come; In the scroll of the book it is written of me.
I delight to do Your will, O my God;
Your Law is within my heart." Psalm 40:7, 8

Stringing Along

10 months

Equipment: a pull-toy or a toy and a piece of cord or shoelace

James 4:8 says, "Draw near to God and He will draw near to you." In this simple activity Baby will be learning to draw an object nearer. The tendency is to think of pull-toys as toys for children who are already walking; but in this project it is almost better if Baby isn't on foot yet because he will be more likely to desire a toy he cannot walk to easily.

Have Baby seated, either at a table or on the floor. Place a toy in front of him with one end of a cord attached to the toy and put the other end of the cord within easy reach. Will Baby grab the string and pull the toy to himself? If not, try showing him by tugging on the string and pulling the toy about half the distance in. Does Baby want to take over pulling the cord now? Make a game of it. Baby will soon learn that pulling on the string will make the toy move.

Just as we want Baby to draw the toy to himself, God wants us to draw near to Him. We can't just sit there and have it happen. We need to make the effort.

Let us draw near with a sincere heart in full assurance of faith…
Hebrews 10:22

Shape and Form

10 months +

Equipment: a wooden or plastic block (cube), a ball (sphere) of approximately the same size, and two pieces of heavy cardboard; or a purchased shape sorter.

This activity will help baby organize space at a very simple level. Cut a circle in the cardboard which is just large enough to allow the sphere to pass through. Likewise, cut a square which allows the cube to narrowly fit through it. What you are really doing is making one of Baby's first puzzles. It is simpler to pass the ball through its opening because no matter which way you turn it, it always fits. The block provides a much greater challenge because the corners must be lined up for it to fit.

In Genesis 1:2 we read that the earth *was* without form, but we also realize God did not leave it that way. God's works do have order and form. He made the birds for the air, the cattle for the land and the fish for the sea. Everything has its own place to fit into God's plan.

The sea is His, for it was He who made it, And His hands formed the dry land. Psalm 95:5

Echo

10-11 months

No equipment

Rhema is a Greek word meaning utterance. It refers to a word produced by a voice and having definite meaning. We get a glimpse of how important spoken words are when we consider that God *called* the worlds into being when he *said*, "Let there be light." And there was!

This game gives Baby practice in listening accurately and in learning to control the muscles used in producing speech. Choose a time with no outside distractions. Position yourselves so that you can see each other's face clearly. Repeat a sound that Baby just made or, if he is not talking, pick one sound Baby repeats when he's babbling naturally. Sounds with hard consonants like "buh" or "duh" work best. Say the sound, then be quiet and give Baby time to respond. If he doesn't reply, look at him with your mouth wide open as if you are about to begin talking. Many times he'll imitate your facial gesture and then supply his own sound. Try to create a dialogue of echoes.

...but man lives by everything that proceeds out of the mouth of the LORD.   Deuteronomy 8:3

"Rhema - Greek Lexicon". StudyLight.org
http://www.studylight.org/lex/grk/view.cgi?number=4487 (accessed June 20, 2007).

Accuracy

10 – 11 months

Equipment: un-sharpened pencils or plain clothespins (not the spring type) and a laundry detergent jug with the inner spout removed or other similar bottle.

Things don't always fit in place the way we think they should. Sometimes we have the right pieces to the puzzle but they do not seem to fit. In this exercise, Baby has to turn a long thin object until it fits through the mouth of the container. The most natural grip for babies at this stage is to hold the clothespin sideways, but the jug's opening should be too narrow to allow it to fit like this. Baby discovers that objects must be handled accurately to achieve his goal.

A similar principle applies to accurately handling the word of God. Over the centuries many people have tried to put their own spin on how to interpret scripture and used it as a club to pound in their own beliefs. When the Word of God is handled correctly it will bring life and release from sin. When it is handled inaccurately, it forces or scams people into submission to erroneous ideas.

Be diligent to present yourself approved to God as a workman who does not need to be ashamed, accurately handling the word of truth.
2 Timothy 2:15

Where Is It?

About 11 months

Equipment: any objects Baby recognizes easily, and a few he does not

Jesus came to seek and save that which was lost. In this simple exercise, Baby does the seeking. This easy hide-n-seek game can also reinforce Baby's growing vocabulary. Have Baby seated, either on the floor or in his high chair. Place a block or some other object in front of Baby and ask, "Where is the block?" look left, look right, look up, look down. Each time that you look in another direction ask, "Where is the block?" But don't look directly at the block. Did Baby notice the block? Did he try and get your attention or hand the block to you? Make a joyful and animated fuss when you finally find the block. Try this with other items, naming the objects repeatedly until Baby associates the name with the item.

Finding God often depends upon our willingness to look. And finding Him should be a source for enormous joy. Too often we lose sight of God in the routine of life. Baby's gurgles of delight can remind us that looking has its reward.

When she has found it, she calls together her friends and neighbors, saying, `Rejoice with me, for I have found the coin which I had lost!' Luke 15:9

It's A Ball

11 months

Equipment: a toy ball

Have Baby seated on the rug facing you and gently roll the ball to him. See if he'll respond by trying to roll the ball himself. As soon as baby has grasped the basic idea, you can form a teamwork effort of rolling it back and forth. Take your cue from Baby's reactions and avoid rolling it so fast or so hard that he develops a fear of the ball.

Isaiah 22 tells the sad story of Shebna who was being deposed from office because he failed to rely on the Lord. Rather, Shebna had become proud of his high rank and planned to have a fine sepulcher built as a memorial to himself. But Shebna was disgraced and sent into captivity before he could complete it. Like a whirling ball, there was nothing to stop it. Baby's simple game presents a tough object lesson of how life can quickly become topsy-turvy or spin out of control when we fail to respect God's ways.

"Behold, the LORD is about to hurl you headlong, O man. And He is about to grasp you firmly And roll you tightly like a ball, To be cast into a vast country. Isaiah 22:17, 18

Good Measure

11 months

Equipment: an empty container or plastic bowl and wooden blocks

Many scriptures speak of the fullness and abundance in God's kingdom. In this simple activity, Baby is exploring the opposites *full* and *empty*. Give Baby some blocks and an empty container. Ask him to please put the blocks in his bowl. If he is slow to respond, ask him again while showing him what to do. Explaining any activity as you are demonstrating it will help his language development. When the container is full, exclaim, "It is full!" Then let Baby empty the container and say, "The blocks are all gone. The bowl is empty." Repeat the game.

It begs the obvious, but if Baby puts a lot of blocks into his bowl, he will have a lot of blocks in the pile when he pours them back out. If he puts in only a few blocks, his dump pile will be small. This illustrates the principle that God measures his blessings back to us in proportion to what we have given to Him.

Give, and it will be given to you. They will pour into your lap a good measure--pressed down, shaken together, and running over. For by your standard of measure it will be measured to you in return."
Luke 6:38

The Shell Game

11 months +

Equipment: Two covers (colorful margarine tubs are ideal) and a toy or safe object that can fit under them.

Many aspects of the Christian life involve seeking and finding. We are instructed to search the scriptures, to search our hearts, to seek the Lord, to seek first His kingdom, to seek peace, to seek the profit of the gifts of the Spirit, and to keep seeking things above.

In this activity, Baby will seek the object you have placed under one of the covers. Begin with Baby seated, placing two covers in front of him. Let him watch while you place an object under one of the covers. Then, without moving the covers, ask Baby to find the object. Put the toy under the same cover three or four times in a row and then put the object under the other cover.

Does Baby still look for it under the first cover? At this age, most babies will think the toy is under the first cover where they have "learned" to find it rather than where they saw it put last. Sometimes our spiritual life can become stuck in familiar expectations. Sometimes all we need to find our prize is a fresh outlook.

But from there you will seek the LORD your God, and you will find Him if you search for Him with all your heart and all your soul.
Deuteronomy 4:29

No Other Name

11 months

Equipment: an assortment of various objects

Names are very important. We are identified by our name. This activity gives Baby practice in remembering and identifying the names of common objects, even if he cannot speak their name yet.

Seat Baby in a highchair or on the floor. Begin by placing two objects on the tray in front of him. Speak distinctly and name one of the items, ask him to find it for you. Praise Baby when he finds the right one. As his skill increases, make the game more challenging by adding more objects to his choices.

The world is full of choices; some are proper and acceptable, and others are incorrect. In Deuteronomy 30:15-20, God lays out two choices before us. We are told to choose life. In Joshua 24:15, Joshua challenges the Israelites to choose which God they will serve. He declares he will serve the Lord, the living God. He named his destiny. You can too.

And there is salvation in no one else; for there is no other name under heaven that has been given among men by which we must be saved." Acts 4:12

Expectation

12 months

No equipment

In this game, you will watch to see if Baby can recognize the signals and anticipate the action. Begin by having Baby seated facing you. Dramatically place your hands palms down in front of him so that Baby can't help but notice. See if Baby will mimic you by placing his hands down too; this varies with a child's personality. Choose two or three words to use as a countdown such as, "Ready, set, go!" or "One, Two, Three!" Say the countdown and then quickly turn your palms facing up. If Baby is following your lead, does he turn his palms up too? Continue saying your countdown and flip your hands over again; repeating the pattern several times to establish a cadence and rhythm. Watch for signs that your baby is expecting you to flip your hands over and is able to anticipate when that will happen. This is a very tricky exercise for many one-year-olds; so remember you are playing a game, not measuring IQ.

The Lord wants us to learn to expect good things when we listen to His voice.

But as for me, I will watch expectantly for the LORD; I will wait for the God of my salvation. Micah 7:7

Taking a stand

Varies widely

No special equipment, but check area for safety

One of the most important large muscle skills Baby develops is that of pulling himself up to a standing position. It takes both strength and stability in the legs and trunk, and is a precursor to walking. The best training for this is to just step back and let him try for himself. Give him plenty of supervised, but unencumbered time where he is free to move, free from being strapped into a seat or stroller. Take all the normal precautions of checking for items that could topple over on top of Baby when he pulls on them.

At some point, Baby will become motivated to reach the goal of standing, and then of walking. A whole new level of exploration becomes available once he lifts himself up off the floor.

A maturing Christian will also be called to stand. Standing entails a higher level of effort; the challenge is greater, but so is the reward.

But get up and stand on your feet; for this purpose I have appeared to you, to appoint you a minister and a witness not only to the things which you have seen, but also to the things in which I will appear to you. Acts 26:16

Bye-bye

Varies

No equipment

Waving bye-bye is among the first social skills that babies learn, often participating in this form of social language even before they begin talking. This simple milestone shows that Baby is growing in an awareness of other people who live in his own space and time. It is an early form of good manners. Training Baby to acknowledge another person will also affect the way others respond to him in return.

If you haven't been doing this already, start encouraging Baby to wave good-bye whenever people he is familiar with are leaving. The real accomplishment will be when he initiates waving bye-bye on his own without prompting. Whenever his wave is returned by the person who is leaving, it will reinforce his growing social skills

People are always coming and going in our lives. The more able our response, the smoother our lives will be.

When our days there were ended, we left and started on our journey, while they all, with wives and children, escorted us until we were out of the city. After kneeling down on the beach and praying, we said farewell to one another. Acts 21:5

Appendix

The chief lesson to take from *Bible Lessons with Babies* is that the Spirit of the Lord can be woven into our daily lives. It is about building an awareness of God's plan in simple daily goals and seeing His design in an otherwise ordinary achievement. It is about choosing to create an environment where we are able to feel His spirit standing alongside us.

A child's growth began at conception and continues on without stopping. Training that growth is a continuous task. Likewise, our awareness of God's hand in our child's life needs to be equally ongoing and firm because children do not flourish on the occasional big event; but they thrive on a steady stream of everyday faithfulness.

Morning

Mornings should be a time to greet the new day. Babies should have time to look around, to be greeted with cheery words, hugs, and kisses. Yanking them straight to the changing table and bundling them off to daycare deprives them of those first few minutes of calm morning joy when we reconnect with our creator after a night of sleep. Show your child the delight of the gift of a new day. Healthy digestion requires an unhurried breakfast. Too much stress early in the morning can upset a child's body chemistry for hours.

Midday

Midday is the commerce time in the adult world, and is also the most businesslike part of Baby's day. Its requirements are clear cut: a balance of physical, mental, social and verbal stimulation in safe and loving surroundings. We ought to infuse these times with a conscious awareness of the Living God.

The early physical and mental skills naturally overlap as hand-eye-brain coordination develops. Physical progress occurs when a child uses his muscles. During the first year, Baby needs opportunities to practice building his strength and coordination. Mental stimulation includes the processing of the senses: sight, sound, touch, taste, and smell. The sights, sounds, and textures that Baby encounters can be increased to provide for greater stimulation during periods of wakefulness, and cut back later to prepare for periods of rest.

Social needs during Baby's first year are very simple; mainly one-on-one, or in a very small group. Too many sounds too often from too many people all at the same time are hard for a young child to process. Crowds also bring exposure to many forms of germs and disease, so it is best to reasonably limit the amount of time Baby spends in large groups.

Babies need two different kinds of verbal stimulation. One is individualized, interactive and conversational. This style will ask obvious questions, "Are you wet?" make evident comments, "Here's your bootie!" and will supply words and phrases for

Baby to associate with the objects and events around him. The second kind of verbal stimulation comes from having books read to him or from hearing clusters of longer sentences in context. This helps establish and familiarize Baby with the patterns and cadence of his mother tongue.

Taken together, these activities comprise the business of babyhood.

Nighttime

Research studies have validated what we have long known by intuition; that the thoughts we have just before going to bed stay with us, and that the last words are some of the most potent words of the day. It is this time of day when a child most needs to hear assurances of love, to hear the evening prayers, and to forgive the harshness of the day.

Too often, tired parents miss this most precious time by fighting bedtime battles instead. Too many so-called experts give poor advice based on wrong priorities. The objective is not to get a child to go to bed by himself so the parent can have a half-hour of peace. The objective is to provide that peace to the child so that all the family can sleep calmly.

Some "experts" describe a bedtime training system where the parent begins by sitting in a chair next to the child's bed. Each night the parent is to move his chair a few feet further away from the child's bed, while also reducing the minutes spent doing so. This is *not* teaching a child how to sleep. It is only teaching him to stay in bed. It is *not* teaching him to cast the cares of the day on God. It is training him to survive incremental abandonment. This approach does *not* show parents how to supply their child with security. It weans parents away from listening to their God-given instinct. Both literally and figuratively, it puts distance between parent and child prematurely.

A better way of bedtime is one that is free from harsh and scolding words. It is one that takes the time to evaluate the day; to release the angers of daily small injustices, to heal the small piercings of a child's soul that, when left unchecked, will cover themselves in callousness. It is a time of giving and receiving forgiveness that was not offered during the day.

A good bedtime may have a story of wholesome thoughts to ponder. A good bedtime will have seen to it that all the toys are stowed in their places and all the teeth are brushed. A good bedtime will once again recall the child's heart back to the God who is watching over him. Give you and your child enough time to do it properly.

It might help to focus your priorities if you think of every bedtime as the last goodbye. That chair schooching through the doorway when the stopwatch reached three-minute mark looks pretty silly now, doesn't it? Is that the last image you wish to leave for your child?

At the most fundamental level, a child does not have to be taught to have Faith. God has designed every person to be born with a measure of it. The faith of your child can understand God as well as an adult's. Never underestimate the faith in a child's spirit by looking at the size of his body or the mental processes of his mind. The fundamental measure of faith allows a child to know God. Young children do not have any problem knowing that God exists. If you meet a youth or an adult who questions God's existence, then you are seeing a person who has had their initial measure of faith trained to doubt.

Knowledge that is beyond the basic measure comes from revelation, instruction, and training. As parents or overseers of a child's heart, it is your obligation to train a child's faith; and this is an awesome responsibility. The journey will be unique to you and your child. It will be filed with adventure, and giggles, and sorrows, and a whole gamut of experiences, but ultimately it will end with untold joy when your child loves the Lord.

Jaded adults are often surprised to find that a very young child can understand that God is Love, and that in love he sent a person, his son Jesus, into this world as a Savior. A very young child can understand that Jesus grew up, that he loves children, and that he died and went to his Father in heaven. Very young children can understand that in dying, Jesus made a way that all children may go to heaven some day, but that we have to trust him, and to ask him.

These then are the simple points of early training in faith: To trust in God's love and in Jesus.

Avoid becoming derailed by trivial distractions. Often the goal is bordered in a fine line, but the purpose which parents need to keep clear in their own minds is this: You are training your child to have faith in Jesus; not faith in perfunctory prayer, not faith in church, not faith in rituals, but in the person Jesus. Your child was born with a measure of faith for salvation; direct it wisely.

The Three-Dimensional Nature of Human Growth

The Child continued to grow and become strong, increasing in wisdom; and the grace of God was upon Him.   Luke 2:40

And Jesus kept increasing in wisdom and stature, and in favor with God and men. Luke 2:52

Wooden building blocks are one of the classic standards in children's toys. They encourage creativity, exercise fine motor skills, demonstrate principles of physics, and the list could go on for quite some time.

A simple wooden block also makes a great object lesson. It has three dimensions; height, width, and length; yet it is just one block. A child has three dimensions also; spirit, soul, and body. Unlike the wooden block which lost its opportunity for growth when the tree was felled, a child grows in all three dimensions. Scripture shows us the three-dimensional growth of Jesus in Luke 2:52. And Jesus kept increasing in **wisdom** (that is increase in the soul) and **stature** (that is increase in the body), and in **favor with God** and men (that is increase in the spirit).

When we think of a child growing, it is the growth of the body that commonly comes to mind first. The body grows in age, strength, and stature. Many of the activities in *Bible Lessons with Babies* strengthen a child's developing physical skills. These are vital accomplishments because we live in a physical world.

The second dimension takes in the realm of the soul. It is often thought of as the intellect or mind and it includes the transitory emotions that are reactions to the events going on around us. Again, *Bible Lessons with Babies* offers exercises which help to train a child's mind and encourage intellectual growth.

The body increases in physical strength and size; and correspondingly, the soul grows in wisdom and knowledge. The third dimension, the human spirit, is whole and intact from birth; yet it too can increase in grace and in favor with God. The spirit is the real essence of a person. It includes the abiding emotions such as the love which stands despite circumstances. It is the true character that cannot be faked. Scripture also calls it *the heart* because it is who you are at your core.

For spiritual growth, *Bible Lessons with Babies* is merely a signpost. In God's design, it is the parents who have first honor and first responsibility for guiding a child's spiritual growth. Proverbs 4:23 instructs us to "Watch over your heart with all diligence, for from it flow the springs of life."

Food and exercise stimulate growth of the corporeal body, while information and investigation stimulate growth of the intellectual soul. But the spirit, the heart of man is stimulated to grow through relationships with others and revelation from God. God is able to reveal Himself at anytime, but it will happen most easily and most frequently in an environment where we are watching for it.

That is why *Bible Lessons with Babies* is simply a pointer to spiritual growth. The activities may be beneficial to Baby's body and soul, but the chief goal of the lessons is to give parents and caregivers practice in being watchmen, of watching for God to be revealed in the common everyday places of life. In the end, raising your baby to have a watchman's attitude, of training him to have the expectancy of a seeker of God, is among the best gifts you can impart.

About the Author

Emily Hoffhines is a longtime home schooling mother of three children. *Bible Lessons with Babies* was originally outlined and implemented as a program to empower church nursery workers more opportunity to interact with and minister to the very youngest members of the church. It has now been completely revised and edited to help parents and caregivers bring an awareness of God into everyday family life.

www.ingramcontent.com/pod-product-compliance
Ingram Content Group UK Ltd.
Pitfield, Milton Keynes, MK11 3LW, UK
UKHW021322180426
11947UKWH00015B/1380